COWBOY BLAZE BARTON'S
First Cattle Drive

WRITTEN BY
DONNA BEASLEY

ILLUSTRATED BY
GWEN ROBINSON

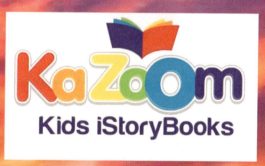

Copyright © 2021 KaZoom Kids Books
No part of this book may be used without written permission of the publisher

Published by KaZoom Kids Books
www.kazoomkidsbooks.com

978-1-7354504-0-7 paperback
978-1-885242-16-7 ebook

"Why can't I go on the cattle drive this year? I'm ten years old now, and you know I'm an excellent rider and good with the cows."

Gramps sipped his coffee and set the mug down on the kitchen table, smiling at me.

"Blaze, your father wants you to wait until you're older. Heck, you're not much bigger than the cows. Being on the trail can be dangerous, and it's a hard life. You'd best be careful what you wish for."

I looked up from cooking the flapjacks and ham, pouting. "Gramps, please talk to Papa for me. I really want to help drive the herd to the trains in Abilene," Kansas."

Just then Papa came through the door, looking tired. He took off his hat and hung it on the peg.

"We just lost our cook," Papa announced. "Boone's horse stepped in a gopher hole and landed on him. Now they each have a broken leg. I can't find another cook by tomorrow morning. Pop, I need you to be our trail cook and handle the chuck wagon."

Gramps' bushy eyebrows rose slowly. "Whoa there, son. I haven't been a cook on a cattle drive in years."

"Pop, if we don't get our herds on the Chisholm Trail before those huge herds come up from South Texas, we won't be able to get to the water holes. There's no time."

Gramps slowly nodded in agreement. "All right, Flint, but I'm gonna need an assistant. Blaze is gonna have to come with me."

It was Papa's turn to look amazed. "What? He's too young."

"And I'm too old. I need his help. Look, I taught the boy how to cook. He knows how I work. Besides, somebody has got to wash the dishes."

Papa was silent for a while. He just sat and ate the breakfast I prepared for him. Gramps caught my eye and winked.

Papa downed his food with some coffee and shot back to his feet. "Blaze, you can come along and help Gramps with the cooking. And since you're coming, we'll take one extra horse plus yours. You'll need to take care of them as well."

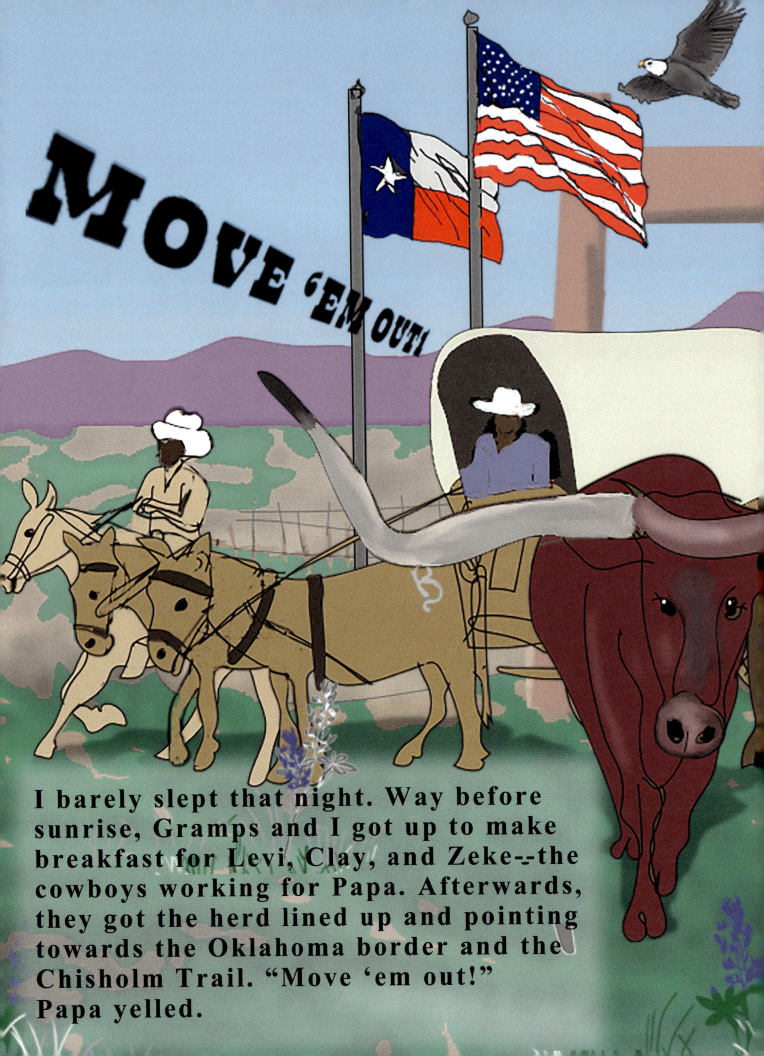

MOVE 'EM OUT!

I barely slept that night. Way before sunrise, Gramps and I got up to make breakfast for Levi, Clay, and Zeke--the cowboys working for Papa. Afterwards, they got the herd lined up and pointing towards the Oklahoma border and the Chisholm Trail. "Move 'em out!" Papa yelled.

The herd started to move slow and steady. There were 600 head of cattle in our herd. They stretched out for about half a mile.

Gramps and I loaded the chuck wagon and hitched up the mules. I tied my horse, Jericho, and the extra horse, Matty, to the back of the wagon, and we rolled out behind the herd. It was a sunny and breezy morning when we left. We were traveling 250 miles from our ranch to the trains in Abilene.

My dog Chaser was barking loudly from the porch, mad I was leaving him behind with the injured Mr. Boone.

The first couple of days were smooth. We were always busy. Gramps made the cowboys meals three times a day. I got up before sunrise to make sure the food was ready for cooking.

Gramps always got the coffee and sourdough biscuits started first thing. He made a pot of beans almost every day. After every meal I washed the dishes with hot water in big metal washtubs.

My teacher gave me two books to read and made me keep a journal
"Blaze, read me some pages from your book while I make the beans," said Gramps.
Every night, after the men bedded down, Gramps lit the lantern so I could write about my day in the journal..

CHASER

One evening, I set up a snare to catch a rabbit. By morning, after breakfast, I had snared us a big one. And the men were stunned when they came in for dinner.

Not only did Gramps make a delicious rabbit stew, he made an apple cobbler.

"If you finished with the dishes," said Papa, "wrangle the horses." My other job was to keep all the horses together and safe during the night. That's why Gramps and I always slept near the horses, so we'd pick up any unusual sounds. But we slept like rocks and couldn't have heard a coyote howling right next to our heads.

After dinner, Gramps always made a campfire and kept a pot of coffee warm. He played his harmonica, and sometimes Levi would sing. Zeke told stories about his army days when he and Papa were Buffalo Soldiers.

On the third day, it rained. It started as a light drizzle, but as the sun set it got heavier. The herd became restless and mooed loudly.

"Oh, it'll be fine," Gramps said when I expressed my concern. Just then, there was an explosion of lightning and a tree was ripped in half.

As soon as the loud boom of thunder reached our ears, the herd broke into a run.

"Stampede!" yelled Gramps. I jumped up and ran. Gramps grabbed me by the belt and yanked me into the chuck wagon. The rumble of the cows grew to a roar. Their eyes were wide with fear as they bore down on us.

STAMPEDE!

"They're going around," I yelled. The wagon swayed from the thunder of pounding hooves as the stampeding cows rushed past us. Both Levi and Zeke were on night patrol. They were on opposite sides of the herd. Papa and Clay quickly saddled their horses and chased after the herd.

"Blaze, get on your horse and get behind the herd. Round up any strays," yelled Papa. Gramps jumped on Matty and rode to help Levi, who was firing his gun in the air, trying to keep the herd from turning off the Chisholm Trail.

I saddled up Jericho and rode behind the cows. I found a few stray cattle bunched together in a ravine. I got them up top and pushed them towards the rest of the herd. One of the cows was too far down for me to reach. I got a rope around her and hooked it to my saddlehorn, and Jericho pulled her up enough so she could climb out.

The next day brought more trouble. The ground was wet and muddy from the rainstorm. The chuck wagon kept getting stuck. We didn't catch up with the herd until suppertime. The men were starving and glad when we got the cook fire going. Muddy shoes, muddy clothes, muddyhorses—a muddy mess to clean up.

On the fifth day, the herd wouldn't cross the watering hole because of the rushing river. The rain had swollen the river, making it too deep. We had to go two miles out of the way to cross the river.

After that everything went smoothly. By the end of the month I could hear the whistle of the train. I knew we were close.

Papa sold the cattle in Abilene. He paid the cowboys, even me and Gramps. We stopped for dinner at a restaurant. It was the only night Gramps and I didn't have to cook.

We slept next to the wagon. Gramps pointed out the Big Dipper constellation in the starry sky. The next morning, we headed home. Papa and I were riding side by side as we watched the sun rise. Suddenly, he turned to me.

"Blaze, you did good work on your first cattle drive."

My lips curved into a smile. "Thanks, Papa." I looked over at Gramps driving the chuck wagon, and he shot me a wink.

SO LONG!

Author's Note: What's the Real Black History?

Blaze Barton's First Cattle Drive is fiction, which means it's a story from my imagination. However, it's based on historical events. Did you know 1 out of every 4 cowboys was an African American? The role of African American cowboys has been largely overlooked in American history books. The truth, however, is the cattle industry would have been severely handicapped if not for the over eight thousand Black cowboys—a quarter of the total number of trail drivers who helped move the herds up the cattle trails. Many of these men were the most qualified top hands, riders, ropers, and cooks. In between drives many of them worked on ranches in Texas and Indian territory.

Made in the USA
Monee, IL
22 October 2023

44717818R00026